This book contradicts the
disagrees with multiple c
led by scripture alone. Y
Matt and Ken" and "The
Protestants (many Pastors) who studied scripture and to...
chaos of Protestant faiths to embrace the truth of the Catholic
Church. May God richly bless you as you seek the truth.

THE MEANING
BEHIND
THE MANNER

A COVENANT UNDERSTANDING
OF THE ASCENSION OF CHRIST

DANIEL DERY

Published by:
JaDon Management Inc.
1405 4th Ave. N. W.
#109
Ardmore, OK. 73401

Cover Design by:
Jeffrey T. McCormack
The Pendragon: Web and Graphic Design
www.the pendragon.net

DEDICATED:

To all who will choose scripture over tradition and engage in the battle for the restoration of biblical [covenant] eschatology, thank you.

> *"Holding fast the faithful word which is in accordance with the teaching, so that he will be able both to exhort in sound doctrine and to refute those who contradict."*
> *Titus 1:9*

FORWARD

In any discussion of eschatology and the nature of the coming of the Lord, Acts 1 and the promise that Christ would come "in like manner" is seen as definitive proof that at some point in the future, Jesus will descend from heaven as a 5'5" Jewish man, in a physical body, riding on a cloud, as the entire cosmos is totally annihilated. These verses are touted as the final refutation of what is known as Covenant Eschatology, or "Full Preterism"; the view that all prophecies stand fulfilled.

In this excellent book, Dan Dery sets forth to answer - head on and with full force - this mistaken interpretation of Acts 1. Dery shows that if (*when*, as most do) the reader is unaware of, or ignores, the covenantal context of the language and the motifs of Acts 1, that this inexorably leads to a total misapplication of the angel's promise. Similarly, when one either ignores or discounts the OT prophetic background and source of Acts 1, confusion is the result. And, when one fails to consider the inter-textual connections between Acts 1 and many other OT and NT texts that irrefutably delimit and define both the nature and the time for the Parousia of Christ in fulfillment of Acts 1, that an entirely false eschatology is created.

As someone that has always been - and still am - a strong believer in comparative charts, let me say that you will truly appreciate Dery's charts that show the perfect parallels between Acts 1 and some key OT and NT eschatological prophecies. These are prophecies that indisputably posit the coming of the Lord in the judgment of Old Covenant Israel in AD 70.

A fascinating and important aspect of Dery's examination of Acts 1 is Luke's use of sacerdotal, priestly, language in regard to Jesus' actions as he prepared to ascend. When one considers this language and imagery Acts 1 will be seen in a totally new light. Finally, Dery shows that you cannot divorce the prediction of Acts 1 from the other NT prophecies of the Lord's final coming from the multitudinous time statements that demand a first century fulfillment. As Milton Terry noted many years ago:

"Whatever the real nature of the parousia, as contemplated in this prophetic discourse, our Lord unmistakably associates it with the destruction of the temple and city, which he represents as the signal termination of the pre-Messianic age. The coming on clouds, the darkening of the heavens, the collapse of elements, are, as we have shown above, familiar forms of apocalyptic language, appropriated from the Hebrew prophets... "To make the one statement of the angel in Acts 1:11, override all the sayings of Jesus on the same subject and control their meaning is a very one-sided method of biblical interpretation. But all the angel's words necessarily mean is that as Jesus has ascended into heaven so he will come from heaven. And this main thought agrees with the language of Jesus and the prophets." (Milton Terry (1898) *Biblical Apocalyptics: A Study of the Most Notable Revelations of God and of Christ*; Grand Rapids; Baker Book House; pp. 246-247).

If you desire to look deeper into the Acts 1 ascension event, perhaps in a way that you have never considered; I highly recommend this book. I assure you that you will be amazed at the wealth of information, the careful exegesis, and the force of the logic found herein.

Don K. Preston (D. Div.)
President, Preterist Research Institute
Ardmore, Ok.
www.donkpreston.com
www.bibleprophecy.com

CONTENTS OF THE BOOK

An Introduction to The Ascension   1-9

Part One:
It was Never About Flesh
Two Conflicting Views   11-14
In Just the Same Way   15-20
Not to Deal with Sin   21-24

Part Two:
Clouds Glory and Blessing
The Covenant Cloud   27-31
Where there are Clouds there is Glory   32-33
A House Filled with Glory   34-35
Temple Construction   36-39
As He Was Blessing   40-43
Ordination of a New Priesthood   44-47
Acts 1:9-11 Fulfilled in Just the Same Way   48-52

Part Three:
***Now* the Lord Has Fulfilled His Word**
A People of Rest, A People who are Blessed   55-58
Not One Word Has Failed of all His Good Promise   59-60
Summary of Conclusions   61

Appendix I.
Acts 1:9-11 Comparative Study   62-69

Appendix II.
The Return of the King - Acts 1   70-79
(Don K. Preston, D. Div.)

Bibliography   80

AN INTRODUCTION
TO
THE ASCENSION

It is my opinion that if we are to grasp the prophetic and covenant significance of the Acts 1 ascension of Christ, the ascension event itself must first be seen and understood within its immediate kingdom and covenant-context. Allow me to explain. At both the close of his first account and the beginning of his second, Luke tells us that for forty days the risen Christ spoke to his innermost circle of disciples, the twelve, of "the things concerning the kingdom of God"; and that he "opened their minds" that they might understand the Old Testament scriptures.

> Luke 24:36-40,44-45
> While they were telling these things, He Himself stood in their midst and said to them, "Peace be to you."
>
> But they were startled and frightened and thought that they were seeing a spirit.
>
> And He said to them, "Why are you troubled, and why do doubts arise in your hearts?
>
> See My hands and My feet, that it is I Myself; touch Me and see, for a spirit does not have flesh and bones as you see that I have."
>
> And when He had said this, He showed them His hands and His feet.
>
> Now He said to them, "These are My words which I spoke to you while I was still with you, *that all things which are written about Me in the Law of Moses and the Prophets and the Psalms must be fulfilled".*
>
> *Then he opened their minds to understand the scriptures.*

Acts 1:1-3
The first account I composed, Theophilus, about all that Jesus began to do and teach,

until the day when He was taken up to heaven after He had by the Holy Spirit given orders to the apostles whom He had chosen.

To these He also presented Himself alive after His suffering, by many convincing proofs, *appearing to them over a period of forty days and speaking of the things concerning the kingdom of God.*

As the Lucan accounts continue, we gain indispensable insight into what Jesus taught during this time concerning the nature of the kingdom, and how his newly enlightened disciples understood it.

Luke 24:49
"And behold, *I am sending forth the promise of My Father upon you*; but you are to stay in the city *until you are clothed with power from on high.*"

Acts 1:4-5
Gathering them together, He commanded them not to leave Jerusalem, but to *wait for what the Father had promised*, "Which," He said, "you heard of from Me;

for John baptized with water, *but you will be baptized with the Holy Spirit not many days from now.*"

In response to this promise, the disciples immediately asked;

Acts 1:6

"…. *Lord, is it at this time You are restoring the kingdom to Israel?*"

Now, regardless of how and to what extent the disciples understood the nature of the kingdom at this point,1 their response should never surprise us. After all, the promise of the Spirit in the Old Testament scriptures is consistently connected to the eschatological kingdom-restoration of Israel.2 And remember, Jesus had just spent forty days "speaking of the things concerning the kingdom of God" out of the Old Testament scriptures. Therefore, in the context of the sending of the Spirit their question was completely appropriate. Below are just two out of many possible Old Testament passages that the disciples would have immediately considered upon hearing the words, "*you will be baptized with the Holy Spirit*". Notice the first:

Isaiah 32:15
Until the Spirit is poured out upon us from on high, and the wilderness becomes a fertile field, and the fertile field is considered as a forest.

In Luke 24:49, the sending forth of the Spirit to "clothe them" with "power from on high", was a direct allusion to this prophecy of Isaiah concerning the restoration of Israel. In its original historical context, this pouring out of the Spirit probably referred to the spiritual [covenantal] although temporal restoration [reform] of the kingdom of Judah under the reign of the righteous king Josiah.3 Meaning, that through the "pouring out" of his power and mercy, God blessed his people through a king [Josiah] who reigned "righteously and justly",4 who "did right in the sight of the Lord, and walked in all the ways of his father David".5 In this way, Israel experienced a typological restoration through the Spirit of

God; when the "wilderness became a fertile field" and the "people lived in a peaceful habitation."6

However, as Luke records, Jesus applied the true eschatological fulfillment of this passage to the pouring out of the Spirit upon the apostles on the day of Pentecost, *a direct result of his ascension.*7 Thus for Jesus, the pouring out of the Spirit on Pentecost, was a definitive sign to Israel that their kingdom-restoration [in fulfillment of the prophets] which he himself had initiated 8 was continuing in and through the ministry of his apostles. Below is the second Old Testament passage:

> Ezekiel 37:1,11,21-28
> The hand of the Lord was upon me, and He brought me out by the Spirit of the Lord and set me down in the middle of the valley; and it was full of bones.
>
> Then He said to me, "Son of man, *these bones are the whole house of Israel;* behold, they say, 'Our bones are dried up and our hope has perished. We are completely cut off.'
>
> "Say to them, 'Thus says the Lord God, "Behold, I will take the sons of Israel from among the nations where they have gone, and I will gather them from every side and bring them into their own land;
>
> and *I will make them one nation in the land, on the mountains of Israel; and one king will be king for all of them; and they will no longer be two nations and no longer be divided into two kingdoms.*
>
> "They will no longer defile themselves with their idols, or with their detestable things, or

4

with any of their transgressions; but I will deliver them from all their dwelling places in which they have sinned, and will cleanse them. And they will be My people and I will be their God.

"My servant David will be king over them, and they will all have one shepherd; and they will walk in My ordinances and keep My statutes and observe them.

"They will live on the land that I gave to Jacob My servant, in which your fathers lived; and they will live on it, they, and their sons and their sons' sons, forever; and *David My servant will be their prince forever.*

"I will make a covenant of peace with them; it will be an everlasting covenant with them. And I will place them and multiply them, *and will set My sanctuary in their midst forever.*

"My dwelling place also will be with them; and I will be their God, and they will be My people.

"And the nations will know that I am the Lord who sanctifies Israel, *when My sanctuary is in their midst forever.'"*

As all students of scripture are aware, one of the most primary Old Testament prophecies concerning the restoration of the kingdom of Israel through the pouring out of the Spirit, is Ezekiel 37. Thus, it would be blindness in the extreme on our part to miss or deny that the disciples had Ezekiel's prophecy in mind when in the context of the coming of the Spirit they inquire; *"Lord, is it at this time You are restoring the kingdom to Israel?"*

Based on this prophetic background, what we see then in the immediate context of the Acts 1 ascension of Christ is the reiteration of the age-old promise to pour out the Spirit that "all Israel" [the whole house] might be gathered together as the dwelling place of God, in which the blessings and inheritance promised to the fathers might be fulfilled.

Although portions of Ezekiel's prophecy no doubt found typological fulfillment in the post-exilic return of the southern kingdom from Babylon to the land of Judah under Ezra and Nehemiah; the entire prophecy was from the beginning Messianic; and pointed to the covenant and kingdom-restoration of Israel under Jesus the Christ. It was through the everlasting new covenant of peace 9 that Jesus the Shepherd-King 10 had poured out the Spirit upon Israel,11 to gather together both kingdoms as one nation in the land,12 that the sanctuary [the temple] of God might be established in their midst forever.13 Undeniably, Ezekiel's prophecy was in the process of being fulfilled in Christ through the forming of the church during the last days of the Jewish age, between approximately 30-70AD.14

At this point you may be asking, and rightly so; how does all this relate to the ascension of Christ? More specifically; how does the immediate context of the Acts 1 ascension [specifically the restoration of the kingdom to Israel in fulfillment of Ezekiel 37] relate to the ascension event itself? In answer to that question, notice just three of the *covenant-elements* found in Ezekiel 37.15

-The *covenant-presence* of God [Ezekiel 37:14,23]
-The *temple* [sanctuary] of God [Ezekiel 37:26-28]
-The *blessings* [fulfillment of the promises] of God [Ezekiel 37:25-26]

Now, consider the following:

-According to Ezekiel 37, the restoration of the kingdom to Israel would involve [1] the return of the covenant-presence of Yahweh, [2] the establishment of the Messianic temple, and [3] the blessings of the promises made to the fathers *applied* to the New Covenant people of God.

-But, the restoration of the kingdom of Israel as foretold in Ezekiel 37 forms the background and context for the Acts 1 ascension event.

-*Therefore, we conclude that the Acts 1 ascension of Christ in some way concerns and relates to the restoration of the kingdom to Israel for [1] the return of the covenant-presence of Yahweh, [2] the establishment of the Messianic temple, and [3] the blessings of the promises made to the fathers applied to the New Covenant people of God, in fulfillment of Ezekiel 37.*

As we shall presently demonstrate, this was precisely the message that the combined apostolic records of the ascension communicated to the first century disciples. *The visible ascension of Jesus served to reveal and confirm the invisible covenant-realities that had at that time begun, and would in that same generation be fully consummated at the revelation of Jesus Christ.* Having established this kingdom and covenant context, we invite you to reason together with us as we seek to unveil the *"meaning behind the manner"* through a covenant understanding of the ascension of Christ.

---

1. It seems unreasonable to me that after having their minds "opened" by the Lord himself for forty days to "understand the scriptures", specifically, the "things concerning the kingdom of God"; that the disciples would still at this point be confused concerning the true and spiritual nature of the kingdom. The fact that they did understand the kingdom as a spiritual rule and dominion becomes evident in the very next chapter [Acts 2], where Peter preaches the rule and reign of Christ [his kingdom] as a then-present reality in

fulfillment of Psalms 2 and Psalms 110. Thus, although the apostles did struggle with certain nuances of the kingdom [such as Jew and Gentile issues - Galatians 2, Acts 15], they clearly did not struggle in their understanding of its spiritual/heavenly nature [Acts 2, 13, 15, Galatians 3-4, 1 and 2 Peter etc.]

2. For example, see Isaiah 32:15, 44:3, Ezekiel 36:26-27, 37:14, Joel 2:28-29, and Zechariah 12:10 in their immediate contexts.

3. 2 Kings 22:1-23:25

4. Isaiah 32:1

5. 2 Kings 22:2, 23:25

6. Isaiah 32:15,18

7. John 7:39, 14:1-3,16-17, 16:7

8. Luke 7:22 in fulfillment of Isaiah 35, Luke 4:17-19 in fulfillment of Isaiah 61:1f

9. Hebrews 13:20 in fulfillment of Ezekiel 37:26

10. John 10:11, John 1:49, 12:13 in fulfillment of Ezekiel 37:24-25.

11. John 20:22, Acts 2:1-36 in fulfillment of Ezekiel 37:5,9-10,14 [and Joel 2:28-32]

12. Matthew 24:31, John 11:52, Ephesians 2:13-18 in fulfillment of Ezekiel 37:11,21-22. It is significant that the kingdom-restoration of Israel foretold in Ezekiel was to be in "their own land", to "the land that I gave to Jacob my servant, in which your fathers lived" [Ezekiel 37:21,25]. The fact that according to Jesus and the apostles, Ezekiel's kingdom-restoration was taking place in their days means that "the land" [Palestine] was being apostolically interpreted to be "spiritual" [covenantal] and not geographical. This definitively defines the restoration of the kingdom to Israel in Acts 1 as "spiritual" [covenantal] and not "natural" [geographical]. Our premillennial brethren have clearly misunderstood the nature of the kingdom of God.

13. 2 Corinthians 6:16, Ephesians 2:19-22, 1 Peter 2:4-5 in fulfillment of Ezekiel 37:26-28

14. Acts 2:16-21, Hebrews 1:1-2, 9:26, 1 Peter 1:20

15. Ezekiel 36 could have been included in this discussion, but for the sake of brevity we have refrained. Likewise, there are many more than three covenant-elements found in Ezekiel 36-37, but again, for the sake of brevity and simplicity we have limited it to three.

PART ONE

IT WAS NEVER ABOUT FLESH

TWO CONFLICTING VIEWS

Many if not all futurists paradigms consider Acts 1:9-11 to be definitive biblical proof that Jesus must yet return to earth both visibly and bodily sometime in our future. But is this belief biblically defendable? Does this belief harmonize with other New Testament passages concerning the return of Christ? And, does this belief honor the established Old Testament usage of common covenant-language so evident in the Acts 1 text itself? Unfortunately for futurists, the answer to these questions is no. Their dogmatic belief is deeply rooted in the false presupposition that the flesh and blood body of Jesus was the primary emphasis of the ascension event.

The truth is, the only way that a visible and bodily future return of Jesus can be supported from Acts 1 is by ignoring every major covenant-element found within the text, and by violating some of the most basic and fundamental biblical hermeneutics. Sadly, the willingness of many futurists to do so has caused a completely unwarranted emphasis on "the flesh", that is, on the physical body of Jesus as it relates to both his ascension and his coming again in glory.

We will demonstrate consistently throughout this work that Acts 1:9-11 in no way supports or emphasizes a future-to-us visible and bodily return of Jesus; but instead, that it powerfully prophesied *the arrival of the covenant-presence of God through the Parousia of Christ, in the lifetime of the first century disciples.* The promise of Acts 1 was not that Christ would *return as man*, but that Christ would *return to man*; that he might establish his Presence in a new temple, his salvation under a New Covenant, and his kingdom through a new people.

Acts 1:9-11
And after he had said these things, he was lifted up while they were looking on, and a cloud received him out of their sight.

And as they were gazing intently into the sky while he was going, behold, two men in white clothing stood beside them.

They also said, "Men of Galilee, why do you stand looking into the sky? This Jesus, who has been taken up from you into heaven, will come *in just the same way as you have watched Him go into heaven.*"

The common futurist argument from Acts 1:9-11 in support of a future and visible bodily return of Jesus goes something like this:

-Jesus visibly ascended into heaven in a physical body.

-But, Jesus must return in "just the same way"16 that he ascended.

*-Therefore, Jesus must visibly descend from heaven in a physical body.*17

-And, since Jesus has not yet done this....
-Then the visible and bodily second coming of Jesus must yet be in our future.

On the surface this argument seems rather convincing, and, if Acts 1:9-11 was the only text in the New Testament which prophesied Christ's Parousia, it would be. But it's not, not by a long shot. As a matter of fact, notice just one passage among many that at face value teaches the exact opposite of the futurist interpretation of Acts 1:9-11.

Matthew 16:27-28
For *the Son of Man is going to come in the glory of His Father with His angels,* and will then repay every man according to his deeds.

Truly I say to you, *there are some of those who are standing here who will not taste death until they see the Son of Man coming in His kingdom.*

In this passage, Jesus undeniably placed his Parousia, this is, his "second coming",18 within the lifetime of his own contemporary generation. Thus, while seeking to honor the *element of time* present in Matthew 16:27-28, the basic "preterist argument" from Acts 1:9-11 in support of a spiritual [non-bodily/fleshly] second coming of Christ goes something like this:

-Jesus promised that his second coming would occur within the lifetime of *some* of his contemporary disciples. [Matthew 16:27-28
-biblical fact]

-But, *all* his contemporary disciples have physical died. [historical fact]

-*Therefore, the second coming of Christ must have already taken place.* [logical conclusion]

-And, since Jesus does not presently dwell on earth in his incarnate flesh and blood body.... 19

-*Then the second coming of Christ must have occurred spiritually [the return of His covenant-presence) rather than naturally (the return of his physical flesh and blood body].*

The obvious problem is that both arguments can't be true. The futurist and the preterist positions can't both be correct concerning the time and the nature of the second coming of Christ as prophesied in Acts 1. Therefore, one of these arguments is false; but which one? Perhaps the following words of the late Milton S. Terry will help to point us in the proper direction. Terry says; *"The obscure texts must be interpreted in light of those which are plain and positive."*20

No honest student of the scriptures would deny the validity of this simple but profound hermeneutic, yet this is precisely what many have done when it comes to the Acts 1 ascension. As we will presently show, "in just the same way" is not nearly as "plain and positive" as many futurists have plainly and positively insisted.

---

16. Translated as "in like manner" in the KJV, hence the title of the book, *"The Meaning Behind the Manner"*.

17. For example, this is the position and argument [in principle] of David Guzik [*Study Guide for Acts 1*], Jamieson, Fausset & Brown [*Commentary on Acts 1*], and John Peter Lange [*A Commentary of the Holy Scriptures*].

18. For an exhaustive study demonstrating that Matthew 16:27-28 did in fact prophesy the second coming of Christ in fulfilment of both Old and New Testament prophecy, see the author's book, *"The Case for the Second Coming of Christ, An Investigation into the Biblical Evidence"*, [Ardmore, Oklahoma; JaDon Management, 2019].

19. It is commonly claimed by futurists that Jesus will return in a "glorified" physical body, citing Philippians 3:21 as a proof text. Unfortunately for them, this claim does not harmonize with their hyper-literal interpretation of *"in just the same way"* [in like manner] in Acts 1:11. Scripture is clear that Jesus ascended in his *unglorified flesh and blood body*, that is, the same flesh and blood body that was both crucified and raised the third day. [John 7:39, 20:17,25-27]

20. Milton S. Terry, *Biblical Hermeneutics*, p.457.

IN JUST THE SAME WAY

To understand both the emphasis of the ascension and the nature of the second coming as prophesied in Acts 1, we must begin by briefly examining the Greek words "houtos tropos" translated "in just the same way" in the NASB version.

> Acts 1:11
> This Jesus, who has been taken up from you into heaven, will come *in just the same way* [houtos tropos] as you have watched Him go into heaven."

According to Thayer's Greek Lexicon, "houtos" can mean "in this manner, thus, so, likewise" etc., while "tropos" can mean, "a manner, way, fashion, even as, like as". What these definitions tell us is that "houtos tropos" *does not have to mean in precisely, specifically, or exactly the same way*. In other words, just because the disciples had watched Jesus ascend in a physical body, doesn't mean that he must return in a physical body simply because they were told he would come in *"just the same way"*. This position can easily be vindicated by a brief examination of how these words are used and understood elsewhere in the New Testament. Let's begin with Paul's second letter to Timothy.

> 2 Timothy 3:8
> *Just as* [houtos tropos] Jannes and Jambres opposed Moses, so these men also oppose the truth, men of depraved mind, rejected in regard to the faith.

Some commentators 21 believe that Jannes and Jambres were two of the magicians in Egypt who opposed Moses by performing similar miracles when Yahweh was pleading with

Pharaoh to "let his people go".22 Recall specifically that when Moses threw down his staff and it became a serpent, the magicians of Egypt did likewise, and in this way *opposed* Moses.23 Paul's analogy between Jannes and Jambres and the men of his day who *opposed* the truth of the gospel illustrates our point quite nicely.

Was Paul saying that the depraved men of his day were doing *exactly* what Jannes and Jambres had done in Moses' day? Were these men turning staffs into snakes in opposition to the gospel? The obvious answer is no. Paul's point was, *just as* [houtos tropos] the purpose of God to deliver Israel from physical bondage was opposed in Moses' day, God's purpose to deliver the remnant from the bondage of sin and death through the gospel of Christ was being opposed in his day also. Clearly, "houtos tropos" in 2 Timothy 3:8 can't be forced to mean *exactly the same way* in a hyper-literal sense. It is therefore best [and most natural] to understand *"just as"* [houtos tropos] in this passage to refer to the "big picture"; that is, to a general/common truth, rather than to an identical or minute detail. Let's look at another.

> Acts 15:7,11
> After there had been much debate, Peter stood up and said to them, "Brethren, you know that in the early days God made a choice among you, that by my mouth the Gentiles would *hear the word of the gospel and believe.*
>
> But we believe that we are saved through the grace of the Lord Jesus, *in the same way* [houtos tropos] as they also are."

Ask yourself again, was Peter emphasizing "generals" or "specifics" in this passage? Did Peter mean that the Gentiles were being saved in exactly, specifically, and precisely "the

16

same way" [houtos tropos] that the Jews were? Did Peter mean that both Jews and Gentiles were being saved *in the exact same places, at the exact same times, and under the exact same circumstances?* Or, did Peter simply mean that both Jew and Gentile were "in the same way" [houtos tropos], that is, with no distinction to race, being cleansed in heart by faith by receiving the gospel?24 The truth could not be more obvious. Like Paul, Peter was communicating a common truth rather than emphasizing specific or identical details. The same is true in Acts 1. The two men in white were not predicting the fleshly return of Jesus in *exactly and precisely just the same way* that the disciples had seen him go. Just like Peter and Paul, their words "in just the same way" [houtos tropos] painted a much broader covenant-picture.

What should also be noticed although not overly emphasized, is that there is absolutely no mention of *"the body"* of Jesus anywhere in the text. Now please understand; I'm not arguing that Acts 1:9-11 can't refer to a visible bodily return of Jesus simply because the word "body" isn't found in the text. That's a terrible hermeneutic, one which I do not endorse. My point is simply this; if the emphasis of Acts 1:9-11 really and truly centers on the bodily ascension and the bodily return of Jesus, then why is there absolutely no emphasis on *his body* within that passage?

Furthermore, why do all "second coming texts" [and even the parallel "ascension texts"]25 within the New Testament also fail to emphasize *the body* of Jesus? After all, if the second coming of Christ prophesied at the ascension is all about his bodily return to earth in a physical/visible manner, then we should expect to find that specific truth permeating the pages of scripture; yet we do not. Acts 1:9-11 basically stands alone as the sole biblical passage which supposedly supports this widespread futurist view. And concerning building doctrines on single obscure passages, Terry has wisely said; *"No single* *statement or obscure passage of one book can be allowed to set aside a doctrine which is clearly established by many passages".*26 I could not agree more.

The fact is for futurists, the problem of the non-emphasis of the body of Jesus in Acts 1:9-11 is just the tip of the proverbial iceberg. For example, if the second coming of Christ is supposed to occur in *exactly the same way* that he ascended, then what are we to make of numerous other passages *which describe that very same event in completely different ways?* To put it plainly, the hyper-literal interpretation of "in just the same way" [houtos tropos] employed by most if not all futurists leads to a blatant contradiction of scripture. Notice, the bible tells us that the second coming of Christ would be:

In judgment, to reward every man according to his deeds….

> Matthew 16:27
> "For *the Son of Man is going to come* in the glory of His Father with His angels *and will then repay every man according to his deeds"*

With the voice of the archangel and the trumpet of God….

> 1 Thessalonians 4:16
> "For *the Lord Himself will descend* from heaven with a shout, *with the voice of the archangel and with the trumpet of God…"*

With his mighty angels in flaming fire….

> 2 Thessalonians 1:7
> "…when *the Lord Jesus will be revealed* from heaven *with His mighty angels in flaming fire"*

In view of "every eye" ....

Revelation 1:7
"Behold, *he is coming* with the clouds, and *every eye will see him....*"

And, as a conquering King, riding on a white horse....

Revelation 19:11-16
"And I saw heaven opened, and behold, *a white horse, and He who sat on it is called Faithful and True...*"

Is it not self-evident that when the disciples watched Jesus ascend into heaven, it was not *in just the same way* [according to the futurist definition] as any of these passages indicate? The disciples did not see Jesus ascend at the judgment of every man, nor in the glory of his Father, nor in the presence of his mighty angels. There was no flaming fire, no voice of the archangel, no trumpet of God. And most assuredly, Jesus did not ascend riding a white horse as King of Kings and Lord of Lord, in the sight of "every eye", even "those who pierced him".27

Clearly, the futurist interpretation of "in just the same way" [houtos tropos] in Acts 1:11 leads to a blatant contradiction of scripture as well as a denial of established prophetic timelines, and must therefore be rejected as the correct interpretation. As we shall see, the emphasis of the ascension was never on the natural body of Jesus, but on *what the covenant-return of Jesus would accomplish for the spiritual Body of Christ.*

---

21. For example, Matthew Henry: *Commentary on 2 Timothy 3*, BLB
22. Exodus 5:1, 10:3-4
23. Exodus 7:10-11

24. Acts 15:9
25. Mark 16:19, Luke 24:50-51, 1 Timothy 3:16 etc.
26. Milton S. Terry, *Biblical Hermeneutics*, p.457. Contrary to the common futurist dogmas, a non-bodily/natural [yet literal] second coming of Jesus can be proven to be biblically accurate based upon it's *clearly established first century time limitation,* found on *many pages of scripture.*
27. Zechariah 12:10, John 19:37, Revelation 1:7

NOT TO DEAL WITH SIN

To add insult to injury, when futurists insist that Jesus must return to earth "according to the flesh"28 at some point in our future, they are unwittingly denying the biblical expectation of the second coming of Christ; namely, *the covenant-return of Christ as Deity.* The Parousia was to be the "Revelation of Jesus Christ"29 *in the glory of his Father,*30 as King of Kings and Lord of Lords.31 Like the Jews of old, much of Christianity today has missed this glorious appearing.

Prior to his incarnation existence, Jesus existed as God 32 and shared equally in the glory of his Father.33 Through his incarnation experience, he emptied himself of that glory and was made in the likeness of men.34 He died, was buried, was raised on the third day and ascended in the same flesh and blood body he was born in. In other words, Jesus ascended in a de-glorified state, that is, in his resurrected incarnation-body.35 Therefore, if Jesus must return in literally *just the same way* as his disciples watched him go [as futurists insist], then Jesus *must* return in the same flesh and blood body that he ascended in.36 The popular yet unbiblical doctrine of a future and bodily return of Jesus, promotes the false expectation of a re-revelation of Christ *as man* and not God. The incarnation-body prepared for Jesus was to put away sin by the sacrifice of himself.37 The second coming 38 of Christ was not to deal with sin [a body therefore being unnecessary], but to bring salvation for those who were eagerly waiting.

Furthermore, the idea that Jesus must return in "the flesh"39 suggests that Jesus must "enter again" [a second time] the lower [earthly] realm of "flesh and blood"40 from which he forever departed when he rose from the dead. Jesus was "born under the law" [under the Old Covenant system]41 and "came into the world" from the Father.42 Meaning that through natural birth, Jesus in his incarnation-body entered the world of humanity, and specifically, the Old Covenant-world of Israel. But, upon completion of his incarnation-ministry, he would to return to His Father, beginning in the realm of Spirit.

Through his death and resurrection in Jerusalem, Jesus experienced a "covenant-exodus",43 a departure from one covenant-world into another, from one mode of existence to another. As the second Adam, Jesus was raised [born again] as the "firstborn" and the "beginning" of God's New Covenant-creation.44 He who was "put to death in the flesh" [died physically under the Old Covenant age] was made alive in the Spirit [raised immortal in the power and age of the New Covenant] forevermore.45 Thus, the ascension of Jesus and the departure of his natural body from earth [the realm of flesh] into heaven [the realm of Spirit] was the physical/natural counterpart of what had already been accomplished spiritually through his resurrection. This was precisely what his *"coming in the glory of the Father"* was all about. Jesus was not to return to the Old Covenant-world of flesh "in the flesh" [in a physical body], but to the perfected New Covenant-world of Spirit "in the Spirit" [through the return of his covenant-presence] to make his spiritual abode among men, revealed in the glory and power of his Father.46

In conclusion, to argue for a future bodily return of Jesus from Acts 1:9-11 based on the phrase "in just the same way" [houtos tropos], is to force an unwarranted and most contradictory meaning upon the text; especially in view of other second coming passages. Furthermore, a fleshly return of Jesus denies a fundamental purpose of the Parousia; namely, the revelation of Christ as God, that is, as Yahweh of the Hebrew scriptures. As we shall now demonstrate, the emphasis of Acts 1:9-11 was not so much on *the manner* that Jesus ascended, but on *what that manner meant* in the minds of those who saw it.

22

28. Romans 1:3, 2 Corinthians 5:16
29. Revelation 1:1, 1 Corinthians 1:7, 2 Thessalonians 1:7, 1 Peter 1:7,13, 4:13
30. See Don K. Preston's book, *"Like Father Like Son on Clouds of Glory"* for an in-depth study on the significance of the phrase, "in the glory of the Father".
31. Deuteronomy 10:17, John 1:1-14, Revelation 19:16
32. John 1:1-2,14
33. John 17:5, Philippians 2:6
34. Philippians 2:7-8
35. John 7:39, 20:17,25-27 Luke 24:39-43
36. It is clearly wrong for futurists to argue that the resurrection of Jesus was his glorification in the fullest sense. According to Acts 13:26-33 and Hebrews 5:5-10 [as well as its Old Testament sources - Psalm 2 and Psalm 110], the re-glorification of Jesus took place *following his ascension at his enthronement as king-priest at the right hand of his Father.* Thus, the glorifying of Jesus was his consecration and designation as King and High-Priest on Mount Zion [Psalm 2:6-7 and Psalm 110:1-2,4]. The second coming of Christ was to both *reveal* and *apply* the blessings of that reality.
37. Hebrews 9:26, 10:5-7
38. Hebrews 9:28. This verse neither mentions a "second coming" or a "second time", as the words "time" and "coming" are not in the original Greek text. How it literally reads is, "shall appear out of second". In the day of atonement context of Hebrews 9 this makes perfect sense. Jesus as high priest, would appear from the "second" [most holy place] to bring salvation to the awaiting congregation. My appreciation to Sam Dawson for pointing this out to me.
39. In scripture, "the flesh" carries both *natural* [fleshly, pun intended] and *spiritual* [covenantal] connotations. [Compare Romans 1:3, 9:3-5, 1 Corinthians 10:18 with Romans 7:7, 8:8, Galatians 3:3]
40. 1 Corinthians 15:50
41. Galatians 4:4
42. John 16:27-28

23

43. Luke 9:31. The Greek word for "departure" [decease in the KJV] is "exodos" which means, "a departure" or as the Greek suggests, an exodus. Jesus' death and resurrection was his exodus [his departure] out of one covenant-world [age] and into another; the "age to come" [the Most Holy Place of the New Covenant] that the New Testament writers were anticipating. Jesus as the "forerunner" [Hebrews 6:20] was the first to accomplish this exodus. What Jesus accomplished for himself in 3 days, he fully accomplished for his church in 40 years [30-70AD.]

44. Romans 8:29, Colossians 1:15,18, Revelation 1:5, 3:14

45. 1 Peter 3:18

46. Jesus made it abundantly clear during his earthly ministry that his "coming" [His Parousia - the arrival of his presence] in great power and glory was to be revealed through the judgment and destruction of first century Old Covenant Jerusalem in AD70. [Matthew 16:27-28, 26:64, 24:2-3,29-34, Luke 21:5-7,20-32, etc.]

PART TWO

CLOUDS, GLORY
AND BLESSING

THE COVENANT CLOUD

I suggest and will now attempt to show, that the meaning behind the manner in which Jesus ascended is found primarily within the common Jewish understanding of three Old Covenant-elements present at the ascension event; namely, *the cloud, the glory, and the blessing.*47 As we shall see, the focus was never on the body in the cloud, but on *the cloud* that received the body. Below is our Acts 1 passage once again....

> Acts 1:9,11
> And after he had said these things, he was lifted up while they were looking on, and *a cloud received him out of their sight.*
>
> They also said, "Men of Galilee, why do you stand looking into the sky? This Jesus, who has been taken up from you into heaven, *will come in just the same way as you have watched Him go into heaven.*"

I suggest it is the *covenant significance of the cloud* that begins to identify the meaning of both the ascension and the coming again of Christ. It was in a cloud that they had *watched* him go, so in a cloud [in just the same way] they would see him return.48 Now, rather than jumping to any carnal conclusions as to what kind of cloud this might have been [cumulus, cirrus, stratus etc.]; we need to think Old Testament, we need to think Sinai, we need to think temple; but most of all, we really need to think *the return of the covenant-presence of Yahweh.*

Below are two Old Testament passages concerning this "heavenly cloud" which may help 21st century Christians understand how 1st century Jews would have processed the ascension event.

Exodus 19:9-11,18

The Lord said to Moses, *"Behold, I will come to you in a thick cloud,* so that the people may hear when I speak with you and may also believe in you forever."* Then Moses told the words of the people to the Lord.

The Lord also said to Moses, "Go to the people and consecrate them today and tomorrow, and let them wash their garments;

and let them be ready for the third day, for on the third day *the Lord will come down on Mount Sinai in the sight of all the people.*

Now *Mount Sinai was all in smoke because the Lord descended upon it in fire; and its smoke ascended like the smoke of a furnace,* and the whole mountain quaked violently.

Exodus 24:16-18

The glory of the Lord rested on Mount Sinai, and the cloud covered it for six days; and on the seventh day He called to Moses *from the midst of the cloud.*

And to the eyes of the sons of Israel the appearance of *the glory of the Lord* was like a consuming fire on the mountain top.

Moses entered the midst of the cloud as he went up to the mountain; and Moses was on the mountain forty days and forty nights.

Those who saw the ascension through the lens of the exodus would have seen that event as a repeat of the Sinai experience. Just as Moses ascended Mount Sinai into the presence of the

Lord *in the midst of the cloud,*49 so Jesus, the prophet like Moses 50 ascended Mount Zion *in the cloud,* into the presence of the Lord.51 But there's more. Both Acts 1 and the events at Sinai occurred in a context of both kingdom and covenant.52 Sinai brought Israel into the covenant of the Lord 53 where they became "a kingdom of priests and a holy nation".54 Through the ascension of Christ the same results were accomplished for the New Covenant people of God;55 beginning on the day of Pentecost.56

The ascension of Christ in Acts 1 must therefore be understood as the heavenly testimony [of which the apostles bore witness] of the enthronement of Christ as King in Mount Zion [the New Jerusalem] for the restoration of the kingdom to the New Israel.57 The cloud which "received him" signified his entrance into the presence of his Father to mediate the new covenant,58 which he had inaugurated with the whole house of Israel.59 This was precisely Peter's point in Acts chapter 2 on the day of Pentecost.60

> Acts 2:34-36
> For it was not David who *ascended into heaven,* but he himself says: The Lord said to my Lord, *"Sit at my right hand,*
>
> until I make your enemies a footstool for your feet."
>
> Therefore, let all the house of Israel know for certain that *God has made Him both Lord and Christ - this Jesus* whom you crucified.

In the context of the ascension, the presence of *the cloud* signified to the disciples [the New Israel] that Jesus was initiating the New Covenant-kingdom and was entering the presence of his Father within the veil. And, as they had seen him go, he would come again *in just the same way*. Meaning, the kingdom he had gone to initiate, he would come again to consummate. Thus, rather than the return of the crucified body of Jesus, Acts 1:9-11 prophesied the coming of the kingdom of Christ in power and great glory.61

---

47. It is no coincidence that these three covenant-elements [the cloud, the glory, and the blessing] are related to the three covenant-elements identified in Ezekiel 37 [the presence, the temple, and the blessing], a primary Old Testament source for the context of the ascension event. Thus, the ascension itself testified to the imminent restoration of the kingdom to Israel as foretold in Ezekiel 37.
48. For example, see Matthew 24:30 26:64, Mark 13:26 14:62, Luke 21:27, 1 Thessalonians 4:17, Revelation 1:7. Significantly, all these passages clearly place the "cloud-coming" [return] of Christ within the lifetime of his contemporary disciples. Acts 1:9-11 being a parallel cloud-coming text, must likewise be limited to a first century fulfillment.
49. Exodus 24:15-18
50. Deuteronomy 18:18-19, Acts 3:19-24
51. Ephesians 1:20, Hebrews 8:1
52. Acts 1:1-8, see our introduction above
53. Exodus 24:7-8
54. Exodus 19:5-6
55. 1 Peter 2:9, Hebrews 12:22-28, Revelation 1:6
56. Acts 2:29-36. Pentecost in AD30 marked the initiation of the kingdom, while the Parousia in AD70 marked its consummation [Hebrews 9:28, 10:36-37, 12:28, Luke 21:20-32]
57. Acts 1:8. This purpose of the "witnesses of Jesus" [to testify of the Kingship of Jesus for the restoration of the kingdom to Israel] is not only vindicated by the immediate kingdom-context [Acts 1:1-6], but from the Old Testament source of Acts 1:8 itself. Acts 1:8 is an allusion to both Isaiah 43:10 and 44:8 which are parallel passages predicting the

gathering of Israel, the pouring out of the Spirit upon them, and the ultimate restoration of their kingdom. [Jesus alluded to the latter in John 7:37-37 and Paul alluded to both in Galatians 1:15-16. Both Jesus and Paul saw these prophesies as in the process of fulfillment through their ministries].

58. Hebrews 9:11-14
59. Jeremiah 31:31, Luke 22:19-20, Hebrews 10:19-20
60. Acts 2:34-36 is a direct quotation of Psalm 110:1-2
61. Psalm 145:11, Daniel 7:13-14, Mark 8:38-9:1, Revelation 11:15-19, 12:10

WHERE THERE ARE CLOUDS THERE IS GLORY

If there were ever two covenant-elements that were inextricably linked in the psyche of the first century Jews, it was *clouds and glory*. At least as far back as the exodus out of Egypt,62 *the cloud* had been associated with *the glory*. But more specifically, it was the presence of the cloud that signified *the presence of the glory of the Lord*.

> Exodus 16:10
> It came about as Aaron spoke to the whole congregation of the sons of Israel, that they looked toward the wilderness, and behold, *the glory of the Lord appeared in the cloud.*

It is no coincidence then that this is precisely the connection Luke makes concerning Jesus' ascension. In Acts 1 he emphasized *the cloud*, in his gospel he emphasized *the glory*.

> Luke 24:25-26,51
> And He said to them, "O foolish men and slow of heart to believe in all that the prophets have spoken!
>
> Was it not necessary for the Christ to suffer these things and *to enter into His glory?*
>
> While He was blessing them, He parted from them and *was carried up into heaven.*

Likewise, while commenting on the ascension event, Paul emphasized the very same thing....

1 Timothy 3:16

By common confession, great is the mystery of godliness: He who was revealed in the flesh, was vindicated in the Spirit, seen by angels, proclaimed among the nations, believed on in the world, *taken up in glory*.63

Thus, by comparing several ascension passages 64 we see that the common covenant-elements of *the glory* and *the cloud*, were a primary emphasis in the ascension of Jesus. And as we'll see next, when the combination of these two elements are placed within the context of his coming [his return]; the meaning becomes extremely specific. In the minds of the ancients of Israel, the *coming of the Lord in a cloud of glory* meant 65 the return of his covenant-presence to inhabit and glorify his temple.

---

62. I suggest that these elements are found as early as Genesis 15:17-18 where God *cuts covenant* with Abram.
63. To be sure, there is a difference between being *"taken up in glory"* and being *"glorified while taken up"*, the former being true of Jesus. The ascension recorded in both Acts 1 and Luke 24 help to interpret 1 Timothy 3:16. Jesus was taken up in the glory-cloud *in order to* enter into his glory, that is, to be glorified through the inauguration of his rule and reign in heaven.
64. Namely, Luke 24:25-26,51 Acts 1:9-11, 1 Timothy 3:16
65. Beyond this "temple application", the combined elements of *cloud* and *glory* in the context of *his coming*, often refers to the covenant-presence of the Lord in both blessing and cursing, to both reward and to judge. [Isaiah 19:1f, Daniel 7:13f, Matthew 24:29-31, Luke 21:20-32]

A HOUSE FILLED WITH GLORY

Beginning in the book of Exodus, Israel's Old Testament scriptures provide the necessary biblical backdrop to properly understand the connection between the glory-cloud and temple, in the context of both the ascension and the coming again of Christ. Consider the following passages....

> Exodus 40:33-34
> He erected the court all around the tabernacle and the altar, and hung up the veil for the gateway of the court. Thus, *Moses finished the work.*
>
> Then *the cloud* covered the tent of meeting, *and the glory of the Lord filled the tabernacle.*
>
> 1 Kings 7:51, 8:10-11
> Thus, *all the work that King Solomon performed in the house of the Lord was finished.*
>
> It happened that when the priests came from the holy place, *the cloud filled the house of the Lord,*
>
> so that the priests could not stand to minister *because of the cloud, for the glory of the Lord filled the house of the Lord.*

Under the headship of both Moses and Solomon, when the building of the house was *finished*, the glory of the Lord, manifested by the cloud, filled the house. Of course, these events being but a shadow of good things to come,66 foretold the greater work of Jesus in a greater and more perfect tabernacle.

As he breathed his last on the cross he cried out, "it is finished",67 signifying that through death his "incarnation work"68 had been accomplished. As a result, the chief corner stone 69 and foundation 70 of the new covenant temple ascended into glory forty days later. The glory-cloud ascension of Christ indicated that the foundation of the true temple of God was finished and about to be glorified. Therefore, the coming again of Christ - in *just the same way* - would be to *finish the house*, and to *fill that house with his glory [presence]*.

Thus, Acts 1:9-11 prophesied the return of the covenant-presence of Yahweh to complete and glorify his temple, the church, the body of Christ. Once again, what Christ had begun through his ascension he would consummate at his Parousia. When we consider the synchronous first century themes of *temple construction* and the *glory-cloud coming of Christ* found within the pages of the New Testament, this conclusion makes perfect sense, both biblically and historically.

---

66. Hebrews 10:1. Literally "about to come", from the Greek word "mello".
67. John 19:30
68. John 5:36
69. Psalm 118:22, Acts 4:11
70. Isaiah 28:16, 1 Corinthians 3:11

TEMPLE CONSTRUCTION

Much like Bezalel, who was filled with the Spirit of God to both perform and teach every work concerning the construction of the tabernacle,71 Paul, according to the grace of God through the Spirit was made a wide "master builder" in the construction of the new covenant temple.

> 1 Corinthians 3:9-10
> For we are God's fellow workers; you are God's field, *God's building.*
>
> According to the grace of God which was given to me, *like a wise master builder* 72 *I laid a foundation, and another is building on it.* But each man must be careful how he builds on it.

And without dispute, the *building up* of the body of Christ in the first century was *the construction* of the Messianic temple as prophesied in the old testament scriptures.

> 1 Peter 2:4-6
> And coming to Him as to *a living stone* which has been rejected by men, but is choice and precious in the sight of God,
>
> *you also, as living stones, are being built up as a spiritual house for a holy priesthood,*73 to offer up spiritual sacrifices acceptable to God through Jesus Christ.
>
> *For this is contained in Scripture: Behold, I lay in Zion a choice stone, a precious corner stone,* and he who believes in him will not be disappointed.74

2 Corinthians 6:16

Or what agreement has the temple of God with idols? *For we are the temple of the living God;* just as God said,75 *I will dwell in them and walk among them;* and I will be their God, and they shall be my people.

Ephesians 2:19-22

So then, you are no longer strangers and aliens, but *you are fellow citizens with the saints, and are of God's* household,
having *been built on the foundation of the apostles and prophets, Christ Jesus Himself being the corner stone,*76

in whom the whole building, being fitted together, is growing into a holy temple in the Lord,

in whom *you also are being built together into a dwelling of God in the Spirit.*77

Therefore, within the context of *temple construction*, the coming of the Son of Man *in the cloud of glory* would have meant only one thing in the mind of the first century church; the return of the covenant-presence of Yahweh to glorify *his finished house*, the body of Christ. The tearing down of the temple made with hands in AD70,78 signified then and still does today, that the eternal dwelling of God is among men in the true and more perfect tabernacle.79 John the apostle gave us a beautiful picture of the identity of the body of Christ; the finished and glorified temple of God Almighty.

Revelation 21:3,9-11

And I heard a loud voice from the throne, saying, *Behold, the tabernacle of God is among men, and He will dwell among them*, and they shall be

His people, and God Himself will be among them.80

Then one of the seven angels who had the seven bowls full of the seven last plagues came and spoke with me, saying, "Come here, *I will show you the bride, the wife of the Lamb.*"

And he carried me away in the Spirit to a great and high mountain, *and showed me the holy city, Jerusalem, coming down out of heaven from God,*

*having the glory of God.*81 Her brilliance was like a very costly stone, as a stone of crystal-clear jasper.

In conclusion; based on what we have seen so far, the glory-cloud ascension of Jesus in Acts 1:9-11 indicated at least two covenant-truths. One, Christ had entered the presence of His Father to be enthroned as King in Zion and thus inaugurate the reign [the kingdom] of God.82 And two, that Christ, the corner stone and foundation of the new covenant temple had been laid and glorified. Thus, the glory-cloud ascension of Christ signified *the beginning* of both kingdom and temple within the realm of the new covenant. His coming again *in just the same way* would bring about *their completion.*

---

71. Exodus 35:30-35
72. The Greek word translated *"master builder"* is "architekton", from which the word architect comes. Paul was the chief apostolic instructor - *an architect* - in the building up of the body of Christ, the Lord's temple.
73. In fulfillment of Exodus 19:6
74. In fulfillment of Isaiah 28:16

75. In fulfillment of Leviticus 26:12, Ezekiel 37:27
76. In fulfillment of Psalm 118:19-22
77. In fulfillment of 2 Samuel 7:12-13
78. Matthew 24:2-3,34 Luke 21:20-24,32 2 Corinthians 5:1-5 Hebrews 9:24, Revelation 11:1-2,13
79. Hebrews 9:11, 2 Corinthians 5:1-5, Revelation 21:1-3
80. In fulfillment of Ezekiel 37:26-28
81. In fulfillment of Jesus' prayer in John 17, specifically verses 20-26
82. This point is confirmed by the immediate context of "kingdom restoration" in Acts 1:6-8, as well as it's parallel in Luke 24:49. Luke 24:49 is a direct quotation of Isaiah 32:15, a prophecy of Israel's kingdom-restoration.

AS HE WAS BLESSING

We will now identify the third and final covenant-element emphasized at the ascension event. I believe this element, perhaps more than the others, helps us to understand both *the purpose and the nature* of the second coming of Christ as prophesied in Acts 1. Although this passage is parallel to the ascension as recorded in Acts, the emphasis here is quite different. Notice, Luke records twice that Jesus *"blessed"* his disciples. But more specifically, it was *as he was carried up [as he ascended] that he blessed them*.

> Luke 24:49-51
> And behold, I am sending forth the promise of My Father upon you; but you are to stay in the city until you are clothed with power from on high."
>
> And He led them out as far as Bethany, and *He lifted up His hands and blessed them.*
>
> *While He was blessing them,* He parted from them and was *carried up into heaven.*

And remember, as they had seen him go, he was going to come again in "just the same way". This means that the second coming Christ would bring *a blessing* upon his disciples. According to the writer of Hebrews, *the coming again of Christ with blessing,* would be his *appearing again for salvation.*

> Hebrews 9:28
> So Christ also, having been offered once to bear the sins of many, *will appear a second time for salvation* without reference to sin, *to those who eagerly await Him.*

Peter echoed the identical truth in his first epistle. The grace of God, that is, his salvation, would be received at the revelation of Jesus Christ. He was coming again to *bless them* through the *salvation of their souls.*

> 1 Peter 1:10-13
> Obtaining as the outcome of your faith *the salvation of your souls. As to this salvation,* the prophets who prophesied of *the grace that would come to you* made careful searches and inquiries, seeking to know what person or time the Spirit of Christ within them was indicating as He predicted the sufferings of Christ and *the glories to follow.*
>
> It was revealed to them that *they were not serving themselves, but you,* in these things which now have been announced to you through those who preached the gospel to you by the Holy Spirit sent from heaven - things into which angels long to look.
>
> Therefore, prepare your minds for action, keep sober in spirit, *fix your hope completely on the grace to be brought to you at the revelation of Jesus Christ.*

According to Hebrews 9, both the ascension and the appearing again of Christ pertained to the day of atonement ceremony in fulfillment of Leviticus 16.

> Hebrews 9:11-12,24
> But *when Christ appeared as a high priest of the good things to come, He entered through the greater and more perfect tabernacle, not made with hands,* that is to say, not of this creation;

41

and not through the blood of goats and calves, but *through His own blood, He entered the holy place once for all, having obtained eternal redemption.*

For Christ did not enter a holy place made with hands, a copy of the true one, *but into heaven itself, now to appear in the presence of God for us.*83

Thus, the ascension of Christ signified *his appearing* as God's High Priest in the most holy place to offer his own blood for the sins of the people, *guaranteeing the blessings* of a better covenant.84 The second coming of **Christ** with salvation, was his *re-appearing from the most holy place* to complete the day of atonement, and *fully apply the blessings* of the consummated New Covenant.

Hebrews 9:28
So Christ also, having been offered once to bear the sins of many, *will appear a second time for salvation* without reference sin, *to those who eagerly await Him.*

In fact, it is in this day of atonement context that "the cloud" in Acts 1 takes on even greater covenant-significance. Notice that in Leviticus 16, not even the high priest could enter inside the veil [the most holy place] *apart from the cloud;* lest he die....

Leviticus 16:2,13
The Lord said to Moses: "Tell your brother Aaron that *he shall not enter at any time into the holy place inside the veil,* before the mercy seat which is on the ark, *or he will die; for I will appear in the cloud over the mercy seat.*

> He shall put the incense on the fire before the
> Lord, *that the cloud of incense may cover the mercy seat*
> *that is on the ark of the testimony, otherwise he will die.*

It was therefore fitting that Christ as high priest, also appear before the Lord *in the cloud*. This of course was accomplished when he ascended to the right hand of the Father entering within the veil. And in a "very little while" Christ would come again with the clouds of heaven to bring many sons to glory, granting access within that veil.[85]

> Hebrews 10:36-37
> For you have need of endurance, so that when you have done the will of God, *you may receive what was promised.*
>
> *For yet in a very little while, he who is coming will come, and will not delay.*

Thus, Acts 1:9-11 is a prophetic picture from beginning to end [from initiation to consummation] of the high priestly atoning work of Christ in the heavenly temple, the tabernacle not made with hands.[86] His reappearing out of the most holy place fulfilled the "promise of his coming"[87] for the salvation of the soul,[88] which completed the atonement and established eternal redemption.[89]

---

83. In fulfillment of Leviticus 16:14-16
84. Hebrews 7:17-22
85. Daniel 7:13-14, 18,22,27, Matthew 24:30, Acts 1:9-11, Hebrews 2:10, 6:13-20, 10:15-39, Revelation 11:18-19
86. Hebrews 9:11
87. Matthew 16:27-28, Hebrews 10:36-37, 2 Peter 3:4,9,13,
88. Hebrews 10:36-40, 1 Peter 1:9
89. Hebrews 9:15, Luke 21:28, Ephesians 4:30

ORDINATION OF A NEW PRIESTHOOD

There is another significant point we should make concerning *the blessing of the disciples* at the ascension of Christ. In Leviticus 8-9, Aaron and his sons [the Old Covenant priesthood] were presented and consecrated unto the Lord following a period of ordination; *that the glory of the Lord might appear to both them and all the people.*

> Leviticus 8:30-33
> *So Moses took some of the anointing oil and some of the blood* which was on the altar and sprinkled it on Aaron, on his garments, on his sons, and on the garments of his sons with him; and *he consecrated Aaron, his garments, and his sons, and the garments of his sons with him.*
>
> Then Moses said to Aaron and to his sons, "Boil the flesh at the doorway of the tent of meeting, and eat it there together with the bread which is in the basket of *the ordination offering*, just as I commanded, saying, 'Aaron and his sons shall eat it.'
>
> The remainder of the flesh and of the bread you shall burn in the fire.
>
> You shall not go outside the doorway of the tent of meeting for seven days, *until the day that the period of your ordination is fulfilled; for he will ordain you through seven days.*
>
> Leviticus 9:6
> Moses said, "This is the thing which the Lord has commanded you to do, that *the glory of the Lord may appear to you.*

When their period of ordination had been fulfilled and sacrifice had been made, the high priest *"lifted up his hands toward the people and blessed them"*. Then, both he [Aaron] and Moses entered the tent of meeting, that is, the tabernacle.

> Leviticus 9:22-23
> *"Then Aaron lifted up his hands toward the people and blessed them,* and he stepped down after making the sin offering and the burnt offering and the peace offerings.
>
> *Moses and Aaron went into the tent of meeting…."*

Although Leviticus 8-9 does not specifically concern the day of atonement, I believe that this portion of the passage finds at least a partial/initial fulfillment in the forty days between the resurrection and ascension of Christ. During that time, the disciples [the new priesthood] underwent a period of ordination *in preparation for priestly ministry*. The Holy Spirit was given [at least in a preparatory measure], their minds were opened to understand the scriptures, and they began to be instructed in the "things concerning the kingdom of God".

> John 20:21-23
> So Jesus said to them again, Peace be with you; as the Father has sent Me, I also send you.
>
> And when He had said this, *He breathed on them and said to them, Receive the Holy Spirit.*
>
> If you forgive the sins of any, their sins have been forgiven them;90 if you retain the sins of any, they have been retained.

Luke 24:45
Then He *opened their minds* to understand the Scriptures.

Acts 1:3
To these He also presented Himself alive after His suffering, by many convincing proofs, appearing to *them over a period of over forty days and speaking of the things concerning the kingdom of God.*

Thus, during the forty-day post-resurrection/pre-ascension ministry of Jesus, the New Covenant priesthood was being anointed and ordained *for ministry in the Messianic temple* which would soon be under construction; the foundation stone [Christ] having already been raised. But according to Leviticus 9:23, it was not until both Moses and Aaron 91 returned from tabernacle that the *"glory of the Lord appeared to all the people"*; at which time the two leaders once again *"blessed the people"*.92 I believe that this particular part of the passage found its ultimate and true fulfillment on the great day of atonement, being the hope and expectation of the first century church who eagerly awaited *the appearing of the glory of God.* Notice the perfect parallels.

Leviticus 9:23
Moses and Aaron went into the tent of meeting. *When they came out and blessed the people, the glory of the Lord appeared to all the people.*

Titus 2:13
Looking for *the blessed hope* and *the appearing of the glory of our great God and Savior, Christ Jesus.*

Therefore, the ascension of Christ *while blessing his disciples* signified the imminent consummation of the atonement in fulfillment of Leviticus 16, and the inauguration of a consecrated new priesthood in fulfillment of Leviticus 8-9. Acts 1:9-11 did not foretell the appearing of the body of Son of Man from Galilee, but *the appearing of the glory of God through the revealing of the body of Christ*;93 His glorious New Covenant priesthood 94 made perfect 95 through the redemption of Jesus the Christ.96

---

90. The authority, ability, and responsibility to forgive sin [through the power of the sacrifice of Christ] is without doubt a priestly function [Leviticus 4:20, 19:22] and a key of the kingdom of heaven. [Matthew 16:18-19]

91. Once again, even though the ceremonies of Leviticus 8-9 did not originally concern the day of atonement, it is significant that the appearing [manifestation] of the "glory of the Lord to all the people" is connected to the return of *both* Moses and Aaron from the tabernacle. I believe this demonstrates that not until the Parousia of Christ were the ministries [redemptive offices] of both High Priest [Aaron] and Deliverer [Moses] perfectly and ultimately fulfilled. As it is written, "the *deliverer* will come from Zion.... when I *take away their sins*". [Romans 11:26-27 in fulfillment of Isaiah 59:16-21]

92. The ascension of Jesus as recorded in Luke 24:50-51 draws directly from this Old Testament passage; *"... And He lifted up His hands and blessed them. While He was blessing them, He departed from them and carried up into heaven."* This means that according to the biblical pattern, the return of the High Priest [the second coming of Christ] from the Most Holy Place would bring *"the blessing for the people"*, in fulfillment of Leviticus 9:23. Thus, as His disciples had seen Him go, He was to come again *"in just the same way"*.

93. Romans 8:19

94. Ephesians 5:27

95. Hebrews 11:40, 12:23, Revelation 21:9-11

96. Romans 8:18-30, Luke 21:27-28,32

ACTS 1:9-11 FULFILLED IN JUST THE SAME WAY

What places our interpretation of Acts 1:9-11 on particularly solid exegetical ground is the fact that Jesus and the New Testament writers, when prophesying the second coming, emphasize the *same three covenant-elements* that were emphasized at the ascension event.97 In other words, New Testament prophecy specifically and consistently connects *the cloud, the glory, and the blessing,* with the Parousia of Christ. But that's not all. New testament prophecy *limits* that coming, in the context of these elements, to the lifetime of Jesus' contemporary disciples. Said another way, the New Testament writers clearly anticipate the second coming of Christ in *"just the same way"* as he ascended, and place that coming in the lifetime of their own generation. As we shall see, these facts literally demand a first century second coming of Christ in fulfillment of Acts 1:9-11.

In Matthew 16 we see two of the three elements; *glory and blessing.* Christ would come in the *glory* of his Father, and would then "repay" *[reward]* every man according to his deeds. The full arrival of the kingdom, brought the reward/inheritance, that is, *the blessing* of the saints.98

> Mathew 16:27-28
> For the Son of Man is going to come *in the glory of His Father* with His angels, and will then *repay every man according to his deeds.*
>
> Truly I say to you, there are some of those who are standing here who will not taste death until they see *the Son of Man coming in His kingdom.*

Then, in both Mathew 24 and Luke 21, Jesus mentions *all three elements* found in both the Acts 1 and Luke 24 ascension records.

The Son of Man was to come [return] in *the clouds* of heaven, in power and *great glory*, to gather together his elect; that they might *receive the blessing*, that is, *their redemption* through the restoration kingdom of God. And once again, the Lord himself places the fulfillment of this prophecy in the lifetime of his contemporary disciples.

> Mathew 24:30-31,34
> And then the sign of the Son of Man will appear in the sky, and then all the tribes of the earth will mourn, and they will see *the Son of Man coming on the clouds of the sky with power and great glory.*
>
> And He will send forth His angels with a great trumpet and they will *gather together His elect* from the four winds, from one end of the sky to the other.
>
> Truly I say to you, *this generation will not pass away until all these things take place.*
>
> Luke 21:27-28,31-32
> Then they will see the Son of Man *coming in a cloud with power and great glory.*
>
> But *when these things begin to take place*, straighten up and lift up your heads, because *your redemption is drawing near.*
>
> So you also, *when you see these things happening*, recognize that *the kingdom of God is near.*
>
> Truly I say to you, *this generation will not pass away until all things take place.*

In his first letter to the Thessalonians, Paul, by the word of the Lord, taught the exact same thing. Paul expected that the Lord himself would descend from heaven *in the clouds* to deliver to the saints the substance of their hope, that is, *the blessing of salvation.* According to Paul, some of those who were living at that time would remain alive until those things came to pass.

> 1 Thessalonians 4:15-17
> For *this we say to you by the word of the Lord, that we who are alive and remain until the coming of the Lord,* will not precede those who have fallen asleep.
>
> For *the Lord Himself will descend from heaven* with a shout, with the voice of the archangel and with the trumpet of God, and the dead in Christ will rise first.
>
> Then *we who are alive and remain will be caught up together with them in the clouds to meet the Lord in the air,* and so we shall always be with the Lord.

The apostle John saw the second coming event [his coming again in "just the same way"] through the exact same lens. He was coming with the clouds, and his reward [blessing] was with him....

> Revelation 1:1,7
> The Revelation of Jesus Christ, which God gave to him to show to his bond-servants *the things which must soon take place.*
>
> Behold *he is coming with the clouds*, and every eye will see Him, *even those who pierced Him;* and all the tribes of the earth will mourn over Him. So it is to be. Amen.

Revelation 22:6-7,10,12
And he said to me, "These words are faithful and true"; and the Lord, the God of the spirits of the prophets, sent His angel to show to His bond-servants the things which must soon take place.

And behold, *I am coming quickly*. Blessed is he who heeds the words of the prophecy of this book.

And he said to me, "Do not seal up the words of the prophecy of this book, *for the time is near.*

Behold, *I am coming quickly, and My reward is with Me, to render to every man according to what he has done.*

What's significant about the second coming of Christ as recorded in the apocalypse, is that this prophecy is a conflation of the prophecies previously cited. The coming of Christ *on the clouds* [Revelation 1:7] is a reiteration of Matthew 24:30, Luke 21:27, and 1 Thessalonians 4:17; [not to mention Daniel 7:13]. While the coming of Christ *with reward [blessing]* to "render to every man according to what he has done" [Revelation 22:12], is a direct quotation of Matthew 16:27. In reality, these are all parallel passages.

Furthermore, John's time limitation of "soon, quickly, and near" for the fulfillment of his prophecy [Revelation 1:1,3, 22:6-7,10,12] agrees perfectly with Jesus' "this generation", and "some of those who are standing here" [Matthew 16:28, 24:34], as well as Paul's "we who are alive and remain until the coming of the Lord' [1 Thessalonians 4:15,17]. The undeniable fact is this; according to New Testament prophecy, the second coming of Christ was to occur in *"just the same way"* as his disciples had watched him ascend, and it was to be accomplished within the lifetime of the apostolic generation.

In conclusion, the glory-cloud ascension of Christ in Acts 1:9-11 communicated four great truths to its first century covenant-minded audience. Christ had been taken up into heaven in order to [1] *inaugurate the rule of his kingdom*, [2] *begin the building of his temple*, and [3] *impart the blessings of his atonement*. Furthermore, his coming again in "just the same way" would [4] *bring to completion and fulfillment these great eschatological elements.* The second coming of Christ would bring to consummation all that his ascension had initiated.

Therefore, the first century Parousia of Christ has [1] *fully established the rule of the kingdom of God on earth*, [2] *brought to completion the building of the Messianic temple*, and [3] *fully applied the blessings of the atonement, thus glorifying and perfecting the spiritual body of Jesus Christ, the church.* The mystery of God has been accomplished, as he preached to his servants the prophets.99

---

97. This is also true of many Old Testament writers, particularly Daniel. In Daniel 7 [a prophetic source for many second coming passages in the New Testament, including Acts 1], we find the elements of *cloud, glory, and blessing* [the blessing being the saints receiving the kingdom], in the context of the coming of the Son of Man. As we have mentioned several times, these same covenant-elements are also found in Ezekiel 37, a primary Old Testament source for the context of the ascension event.

98. Matthew 25:34

99. Revelation 10:7. The sounding of the seventh trumpet by the seventh angel took place at the second coming of Christ for the resurrection, and was fulfilled in the lifetime of Jesus' contemporary generation. [Matthew 24:30-34, 1 Thessalonians 4:15-17, 1 Corinthians 15:23,50-55, Revelation 11:15-19]

PART THREE

NOW THE LORD
HAS FULFILLED HIS WORD

A PEOPLE OF REST
A PEOPLE WHO ARE BLESSED

We will conclude by citing a passage which beautifully pulls together much of what we have said in this work concerning the glory, the cloud, and the blessing; in the context of the kingdom, the temple, and the second coming of Christ for the restoration of Israel, as prophesied in Acts 1.

As we have already seen, when Solomon had finished the work of the temple the heavenly cloud of glory filled the house of the Lord thus signifying the covenant-presence of Yahweh with his people. This imagery of course pointed to the second coming of Christ with salvation to dwell in the midst of his glorified church. Below is the text.

> 1 Kings 7:51
> Thus, *all the work that King Solomon performed in the house of the Lord was finished.*
>
> 1 Kings 8:10-11
> It happened that when the priests came from the holy place, *the cloud filled the house of the Lord,*
>
> so that the priests could not stand to minister because of the cloud, *for the glory of the Lord filled the house of the Lord.*

Following the glory of the Lord filling the temple, Solomon then began to communicate to all the assembly of Israel what this manifestation of the presence of God *meant for the people of Israel.* In other words, Solomon here explains "the meaning behind the manner".

1 Kings 8:15-20

He said, blessed be the Lord, the God of Israel, *who spoke with His mouth to my father David and has fulfilled it with His hand,* saying,

Since the day that I brought My people Israel from Egypt, I did not choose a city out of all the tribes of Israel in which to build a house that My name might be there, but I chose David to be over My people Israel.'

Now it was in the heart of my father David to build a house for the name of the Lord, the God of Israel.

But the Lord said to my father David, 'Because it was in your heart to build a house for My name, you did well that it was in your heart.

Nevertheless, you shall not build the house, but *your son who will be born to you, he will build the house for My name.'*

Now the Lord has fulfilled His word which He spoke; for I have risen in place of my father David and sit on the throne of Israel, as the Lord promised, *and have built the house for the name of the Lord, the God of Israel.*

Solomon understood that *through the establishment of his kingdom,* the God of Israel had fulfilled the promise made to his father David. The promise to which Solomon referred was a promise given to David through the prophet Nathan which is recorded in 2 Samuel 7:6-16. Notice specifically verses 12-13.

> 2 Samuel 7:12-13
> When your days are complete and you lie
> down with your fathers, *I will raise up
> your descendant after you,* who will come forth
> from you, and *I will establish his kingdom.*
>
> *He shall build a house for My name,* and I will
> *establish the throne of his kingdom forever.*

According to both Peter and Paul,100 this promise found
fulfillment through the ascension of Christ when he took his
seat at the right hand of the Father having received the throne
and kingdom of his father David. This is of course true, at least
partially. Based on the words of Solomon, I suggest that this
promise made to David had only *begun to be fulfilled* at that time.
And here is why....

In 2 Samuel 7, the promise of the kingdom made to David *is
connected to and includes the building of the house of the Lord.* This
explains why that promise found its typological fulfillment *only
after* Solomon had finished building the house. In other words,
only when the house of the Lord was finished would the
promise made to David truly be fulfilled; as Solomon says, *"Now
the Lord has fulfilled his word..."* This agrees perfectly with what
we have established above. Through his ascension, Christ had
both initiated the kingdom and begun the building of the
temple; *yet only through his Parousia [his second coming], would both be
consummated.* And notice, according to 1 Kings 8, it is only in a
finished house [a glorified and consecrated temple] *that the people
of God find rest and the people of God are blessed.*

> 1 Kings 8:54-56
> When Solomon had finished praying this
> entire prayer and supplication to the Lord, he
> arose from before the altar of the Lord, from

kneeling on his knees with his hands spread toward heaven.

And he stood and blessed all the assembly of Israel with a loud voice, saying:

Blessed be the Lord, *who has given rest to His people Israel,* according to all that He promised; not one word has failed of all His good promise, which He promised through Moses His servant.

---

100. Acts 2:29-36 and Acts 13:21-34

NOT ONE GOOD WORD HAS FAILED
ALL HAS COME TO PASS

We must make one final point concerning 1 Kings 8. According to Solomon, the establishment of his kingdom and the completion and consecration of the temple through the arrival of the covenant-presence of the Yahweh, *was the fulfillment of all that the Lord had promised through his servant Moses.* In other words, in its Old Covenant typological form, this historical and covenant-event [the establishment of the kingdom and the consecration of the temple] marked the fulfillment of the hope of Israel, the goal of her prophetic destiny, and *the fulfillment of all that had been written.* This was precisely the covenant-connection made by Jesus as recorded in the gospel of Luke. Jesus himself declared that when the kingdom was established and the saints received their redemption at his glory-cloud coming [the return of his covenant presence to the temple - the church]; that *"all things which are written" would be fulfilled.* And, that "all these things" were to take place within the lifetime of his contemporary generation.

> Luke 21:20,22,27-28,31-32
> But *when you see Jerusalem surrounded by armies, then recognize that her desolation is near.*
>
> Because these are days of vengeance, *so that all things which are written will be fulfilled.*
>
> Then they will see *the Son of Man coming in a cloud with power and great glory.* But *when these things begin to take place,* straighten up and lift up your heads, because *your redemption is drawing near.*
>
> So you also, *when you see these things happening, recognize that the kingdom of God is near.*

> Truly I say to you, *this generation will not pass away until all things take place.*

The judgment and removal of the Old Covenant temple and the enemies of God in AD70 signified the second coming of Christ to glorify and dwell forever in his New Covenant temple [the church] *in fulfillment of all that had been written.* Those events in those last days marked the goal of all prophecy and the arrival of all the blessings that God had promised through his servant Moses.

SUMMARY OF CONCLUSION

We have seen that the kingdom and covenant context of Ezekiel 37 served as a primary Old Testament source for understanding the covenant-significance of the ascension event.

We have seen that the covenant-elements of cloud, glory, and blessing in the context of the ascension, pointed to and prophesied the return of the covenant-presence of Christ [his second coming] to consummate his kingdom, to consecrate his temple, and to apply the blessings of his eternal atonement to his New Covenant people.

We have seen that this glorious consummation as typified under Solomon, would accomplish the true and spiritual fulfillment of the promise made to the fathers, in fulfillment of all that had been written.

We have seen that the fulfillment of all these things must have been accomplished in the lifetime of Jesus' contemporary disciples.

Therefore, through the covenant language and imagery of the Old Testament scriptures, the Acts 1 ascension event both communicated and emphasized to its first century audience that the second coming of Christ in "just the same way", would *fulfill all of the Lord's good promise which he had promised through his servant Moses;* even in their generation. This, we suggest, is *the meaning behind the manner* and the covenant understanding of the ascension of Jesus Christ.

APPENDIX I.
ACTS 1:9-11 COMPARATIVE STUDY

The following two series of charts will clearly demonstrate that the promise made to the disciples that; *"This Jesus, who has been taken up from you into heaven, will come in just the same way as you have watched Him go into heaven"*; prophesied the end of the age Parousia of Christ which He, his apostles, and the Old Testament prophets identified as *the time of Israel's salvation* [the blessing] which they all consistently placed *at the fall of Jerusalem and the judgment of Old Covenant Israel for shedding innocent blood in AD70.* This evidence powerfully repudiates all futurist concepts of a future bodily return of Jesus, and at the same time proves that the second coming of Christ concerned the first century return of the glorious Covenant-Presence of God to dwell among his people, *which the ascension event signified through the common covenant-language of the day.*

Our first chart demonstrates that the second coming of Christ in Acts 1:9-11 is the second coming of Christ in Isaiah 59.

Acts 1:9-11	Isaiah 59:16-21
The second coming of Christ in "just the same way"	The second coming of Christ [59:19-20] [As per Romans 11:25-27]
In a cloud, in glory	In glory [59:19]
With a blessing	With salvation, for redemption, to take away sin [59:16-21] [As per Romans 11:27]
	In vengeance, to bring judgment upon Old Covenant Israel for shedding innocent blood [59:3,7,17-18]

62

-So, unless there are two second comings of Christ with salvation [the blessing] in scripture, then Acts 1:9-11 and Isaiah 59:16-21 refer to the same second coming event.

-But according to Isaiah, the second coming of Christ with salvation would also bring judgment upon Old Covenant Israel for shedding innocent blood.

-Jesus placed the judgment of Israel for shedding innocent blood at the fall of Jerusalem in AD70. [Matthew 23:29-38, Luke 11:47-51]

-Therefore, the second coming of Christ with salvation [the blessing] in Acts 1:9-11 and Isaiah 59:16-21 must have been fulfilled at the fall of Jerusalem and the judgment of Old Covenant Israel for shedding innocent blood in AD70.

The next chart demonstrates that the second coming of Christ with salvation [the blessing] in Acts 1:9-11 and Isaiah 59:16-21 is the coming of the Son of Man in Matthew 16:27-28 and Luke 21:27-32.

Isaiah 59:16-21	Matthew 16:27-28	Luke 21:27-32
The coming of the Lord [59:20]	The coming of the Son of Man [16:27]	The coming of the Son of Man [21:27]
In a cloud, in glory [59:19]	In the glory of His Father [16:27]	In a cloud, with great glory [21:27]
In vengeance, to bring judgment upon Old Covenant Israel for shedding innocent blood [59:3,7,17-18]	In judgment for shedding innocent blood [16:21-27]	In vengeance, to bring judgment upon Old Covenant Israel for shedding innocent blood [21:12-24] [Math. 23:29-38]
To bring redemption [as Redeemer] [59:20]	To bring reward [16:27]	To bring redemption (21:28]
To repay according to their deeds [59:18]	To repay according to their deeds [16:27]	To repay according to their deeds [Matthew 25:31-46 - parallel prophecy]
To establish the New Covenant [59:21]	To establish the kingdom [16:28]	To establish the kingdom [21:31]
	Fulfilled in the lifetime of Jesus' first century disciples [16:28]	Fulfilled at the fall of Jerusalem in Jesus' generation -AD70- [21:32]

Based on these parallels consider the following argument:
-The second coming of Christ in Acts 1:9-11 is the second coming of Christ in Isaiah 59:16-21. [See first chart]

-But, the second coming of Christ in Isaiah 59:16-21 is coming of the Son of Man with reward/the kingdom [the blessing] in Matthew 16:27-28 and Luke 21:27-32.

-Therefore, the coming of the Son of Man with reward/the kingdom [the blessing] in Matthew 16:27-28 and Luke 21:27-32 is the second coming of Christ in Acts 1:9-11 and Isaiah 59:16-21.

-But notice what this means:
-The coming of the Son of Man in Matthew 16:27-28 and Luke 21:27-32 is the second coming of Christ in Acts 1:9-11 and Isaiah 59:16-21.

-But according to Jesus in Matthew 16:27-28 and Luke 21:27-32, and Isaiah in 59:16-21, the second coming of Christ with salvation/reward/kingdom [the blessing] would also bring judgment upon Old Covenant Israel for shedding innocent blood.

-Jesus placed the judgment of Israel for shedding innocent blood at the fall of Jerusalem in AD70. [Matthew 23:29-38, Luke 11:47-51]

-Therefore, the second coming of Christ as prophesied in Acts 1:9-11 is the second coming of Christ with salvation/reward/kingdom [the blessing] in Matthew 16:27-28, Luke 21:27-32, and Isaiah 59:16-21, which must have been fulfilled at the fall of Jerusalem and the judgment of Old Covenant Israel for shedding innocent blood in AD70.

This agrees perfectly with the time limitations found in both Matthew 16:27-28 and Luke 21:27-32; *"Truly I say to you, there are some of those who are standing here who will not taste death until they see the Son of Man coming in His kingdom" .... "Truly I say to you, this generation will not pass away until all things take place."*

The following and final chart powerfully vindicates and illustrates this conclusion:

Acts 1:9-11	Isaiah 59:16-21	Matthew 16:27-28	Luke 21:27-32
Second coming of Christ	Coming of the Lord	Coming of the Son of Man	Coming of the Son of Man
In glory	In glory	In glory	In glory
In a cloud			In a cloud
With a blessing	With redemption, removal of sin	With reward, to establish the kingdom	With redemption, to establish the kingdom
		Fulfilled in the lifetime of Jesus' contemporary disciples	Fulfilled in the lifetime of Jesus' contemporary generation

The next series of charts demonstrates that the second coming of Christ in Acts 1:9-11 is the second coming of Christ to establish the new creation at the time of the resurrection in Revelation 19-22.

Acts 1:9-11	Revelation 19-22
Second coming of Christ	The second coming of Christ [19:11-16]
In a cloud, in glory	In a cloud, in glory [14:14-20, 19:7-15]
With a blessing	For the resurrection and the new creation [20:11-15, 21:1-2]
	Fulfilled "soon/quickly", the time was "near" in John's generation

-The second coming of Christ in Acts 1:9-11 is the second coming of Christ to establish the new creation at the time of the resurrection in Revelation 19-22, this is undeniable.

-But, the second coming of Christ in Revelation 19-22 [Revelation 22:12] is the coming of the Son of Man in Matthew 16:27-28, which Jesus himself placed within the lifetime of his own generation. [See next chart]

Matthew 16:27-28	Revelation 22
Coming of the Son of Man [16:27]	Second coming of Christ [22:7,12,20]
To repay every man according to their works - the resurrection [16:27]	To reward every man according to their works - the resurrection [22:12]
To establish the kingdom [16:28]	To establish the New Jerusalem, the new creation [22:1-2, 22:14,19]
Fulfilled in the lifetime of Jesus' contemporary disciples [16:28]	Fulfilled "soon/shortly/quickly" [without delay], from when John wrote the book [22:6-7,10,12,20]

-Therefore, the second coming of Christ in Acts 1:9-11 is both the second coming of Christ to establish the new creation at the time of the resurrection in Revelation 22:12, and the coming of the Son of Man to establish the kingdom and to "repay every man" in Matthew 16:27-28; which Jesus undeniably placed within the lifetime of his own generation at the fall of Jerusalem and the judgment of Old Covenant Israel for shedding innocent blood. [See 1st series of charts]

This agrees perfectly with Revelation's "cover-to-cover" first century time limitation,101 as well as possibly the most dominant theme of the book; the imminent return of Christ in judgment of first century Old Covenant Jerusalem/Israel [Babylon the Great] for shedding innocent blood.102

Once again, the final chart below vindicates this conclusion:

Acts 1:9-11	Matthew 16:27-28	Revelation
The second coming of Christ	Coming of the Son of Man [16:27]	The second coming of Christ (22:7,12,20)
In a cloud, in glory	In the glory of His Father [16:27]	In a cloud, in glory [14:14-20, 19:7-15]
With a blessing	With reward, the kingdom and the resurrection [16:27-28]	With reward, the new creation and the resurrection, [20:11-15, 21:1-2, 22:12]
	In judgment for shedding innocent blood [16:21-27]	In judgment for shedding innocent blood [6:9-17, 18:20-24, 19:1-3]
	Fulfilled in the lifetime of Jesus' generation [16:28]	Fulfilled "soon, shortly, quickly" from when John wrote [22:6-7,10,12,20]

Based on the above series of charts, we submit the following for your sincere consideration:

-The second coming of Christ in Acts 1:9-11 was the second coming of Christ in Isaiah 59:16-21 and Revelation 19-22, as well as the coming of the Son of Man in Matthew 16:27-28 and Luke 21:27-32. That event was to bring salvation/reward/the kingdom/resurrection/the new creation [the blessing] to the true Israel of God, the church.

-But, Isaiah [the prophets], Jesus, and the apostles either explicitly or implicitly place the second coming of Christ in Isaiah 59:16-21 and Revelation 19-22, as well as the coming of the Son of Man in Matthew 16:27-28 and Luke 21:27-32 at the fall of Jerusalem and the judgment of Old Covenant Israel for shedding innocent blood in AD70.

-Therefore, the second coming of Christ with salvation [the blessing] as prophesied in Acts 1:9-11 must have been fulfilled at the fall of Jerusalem and the judgment of Old Covenant Israel for shedding innocent blood in AD70, just as the scriptures demand.

---

101. Revelation 1:1,3, 22:6-7,10,12
102. Revelation 1:1,3,7, 6:9-17, 11:1-2,8,13-19, 16:17-21, 18:20-24, 19:11-15, 21, 22:6-7,10,12. For the most in-depth study found in the literature to date concerning the identity of Babylon of Revelation, see Don K. Preston's; *"Who Is This Babylon"*, [Ardmore, Ok., Jadon Management Inc. 2016]. Dr. Preston not only demonstrates that "Babylon the Great" is none other than first century Old Covenant Jerusalem, but that understanding the identity of Babylon is necessary for understanding the story of biblical [covenant] eschatology.

APPENDIX II.
THE RETURN OF THE KING - ACTS 1

By: Don K. Preston (D. Div.)

Without any doubt, Acts 1 serves as a key text for all futurist eschatologies. After all, we are told that since the angel said that Christ would come "in like manner as you have seen him go" that this demands that he will one day descend from heaven once again as a 5'5" Jewish man, riding on a cumulus cloud. What is interesting is that virtually all commentators consulted see, expressing it either explicitly or implicitly, that the promise of Christ's coming in Acts 1 will be the time when Christ puts down the last enemy, ostensibly physical death, at the end of time. I fully concur that Acts 1 depicts the "final" coming of Christ, what is commonly referred to as his Second Coming. I likewise concur that it is the promised fulfillment of Psalms 110. I also affirm that it is the return of the Nobleman to judge the rebellious citizens as described in Luke 19. The implications of this connection are profound.

Peter assuredly saw Acts 1 as the time of Christ's ascension to the right hand of the Father (Acts 2:29f). He described Christ's ascension as his enthronement at the right hand in fulfillment of Psalms 110. If that is the case, then the promised coming of Christ in Acts 1 must be viewed as the time when he would come, as King of kings, exercising his sovereignty in judgment of those citizens who had said; "we will not have this man to rule over us." Amazingly, while many commentators realize that Luke 19 anticipated the AD 70 judgment of rebellious Old Covenant Israel for rejecting her king, they then extrapolate beyond that in Acts 1. But to reiterate, if Christ's ascension in Acts 1 is the departure of the Nobleman into a far country, there to receive a kingdom in Luke 19, then upon what hermeneutical basis does one say that the return of Acts 1 is not the return of Luke 19, the time when the King would judge the citizens who said; "We will not have this man to rule over us!" If therefore it is admitted that Luke 19 posits the return of the King to judge his rebellious citizens in AD 70, this serves as powerful proof that the coming of the Lord in Acts 1 was likewise the return of the King to judge his rebellious citizens - in AD 70.

What seems to be missed by so many commentators is that Peter's conflation of Acts 1 and Psalms 110 in Acts 2 means that Christ's promised return of Acts 1 must be the Great and Terrible Day of the Lord of Acts 2:19; 2:40. The outpouring of the Spirit was a sign of the Great Day of the Lord. That is what Joel said in Joel 2, which Peter cited. To suggest that what happened that day was a sign of events not to take place for two millennia and counting effectively negates the force of a "sign." But, it is critical to see that connection between the coming of the kingdom and the outpouring of the Spirit.

Notice that in Acts 1, when Jesus was asked if he was about to restore the kingdom, he told them that it was not for them to know "the times or the seasons." However, and this is critical, he told them:

> "And being assembled together with them, He commanded them not to depart from Jerusalem, but to wait for the Promise of the Father, "which," He said, "you have heard from Me; for John truly baptized with water, but you shall be baptized with the Holy Spirit not many days from now." Therefore, when they had come together, they asked Him, saying, "Lord, will You at this time restore the kingdom to Israel?" And He said to them, "It is not for you to know times or seasons which the Father has put in His own authority. But you shall receive power when the Holy Spirit has come upon you; and you shall be witnesses to Me in

Jerusalem, and in all Judea and Samaria, and to the
end of the earth." (Acts 1:4-8).

It is important to note that Jesus' promise of the baptism of the Spirit prompted the disciples to ask an eschatological question - i.e. about the restoration of Israel - and Jesus repeated his eschatological answer; they were about to receive the baptism of the Spirit. In other words, what they could not know that day was about to be manifested in the fulfillment of God's promise to pour out the Spirit in the last days to restore Israel - to raise her from the dead! In prophecy, the outpouring of the Spirit in the last days was for the purpose of restoring Israel, (her resurrection), for the establishment of the kingdom.

So, since the outpouring of the Spirit was to be a last day's sign of the Great and Terrible Day of the Lord, and the restoration of Israel, the events of Acts 2 prove that Israel's last days were in progress, her restoration was underway, and the Great Day of the Lord was near as Peter expressed it (citing Deuteronomy 32:5f): "Save yourselves from this untoward generation" (Acts 2:40). Like the warning of John as Elijah - see my book, Elijah Has Come: A Solution to Romans 11:25-27 - who said that the kingdom and the judgment was near, Peter well recognized, with the attestation of the baptism of the Spirit, that the end times had arrived. The question is fair to ask: Is the coming of the Lord in Acts 1, which is his return from his departure as the Nobleman into the far country to receive the kingdom (the throne of David), the same as the Great and Terrible Day of the Lord? If not, how does one prove that distinction? Notice the following.

In Acts 1, Jesus promised his disciples that they were about to receive the baptism of the Spirit to guide them as they went to fulfill the Great Commission: "But you shall receive power when the Holy Spirit has come upon you; and you shall be witnesses to Me in Jerusalem, and in all Judea and Samaria, and to the end of the earth." Jesus' promise was actually a citation of Isaiah 43, a prophecy of Israel's eschatological salvation and her Second Exodus): "You shall be my witnesses" (Isaiah 43:10). This is the exact same promise found in the Olivet Discourse, as Jesus spoke: "This Gospel will be preached into all the world, then comes the end" (Matthew 24:14). He promised them that as they went, they would be empowered by the Holy Spirit to withstand the persecution they would encounter as his witnesses (Mark 13:9f). They would preach the Gospel into all the world (oikoumene) "then comes the end." Likewise, in Acts 1, they were promised to be empowered by the Spirit to preach the Gospel: to Jerusalem, Judea, Samaria and to the uttermost parts of the earth."

So, the outpouring of the Spirit was to empower the apostles to be the Lord's witnesses as they preached the Gospel into all the world. And, the Great Day of the Lord was "sign-i-fied" to be near with the outpouring of the Spirit. The question is; upon what basis do we delineate between the promise of Christ's return and the Great Day of the Lord in Acts 2? If these are the same event, then clearly, the return of Christ "in like manner" in Acts 1 is the Great Day of the Lord that Peter urged his listeners to escape when he says: "Save yourselves from this untoward generation" (Acts 2:40).

The following chart may help us to visualize the comparison between Acts 1-2 and the Olivet Discourse:

The Olivet Discourse	Acts 1-2
The Gospel of the kingdom (24:14), the Kingdom near at the time of Jerusalem's demise (Luke 21:20-32)	Will you now restore the kingdom to Israel
Promise of the Spirit (Mark 13:9f)	Promise of the Spirit (Promise fulfilled in Acts 2)
Spirit to empower them as witnesses	Spirit to empower them as witnesses
Persecution as they preached as Jesus' witnesses (Mark 13:9f)	Persecution strongly implied by the word "witnesses" (See Revelation 11)
Gospel preached into all the world, "then comes the end" (to telos)	Gospel preached into all the world, "this same Jesus shall come"
Gospel preached into all the world (Colossians 1:5,23) (The end was near - 1 Peter 4:5,7,17)	Outpouring of the Spirit was a sign of the Day of the Lord... "Save yourselves from this untoward generation" (2:40)

The next chart below shows the comparison between Acts 1 and Luke 19:

Luke 19	Acts 1
A man goes away	Jesus departs
To receive the kingdom	To receive the kingdom
Gives talents (tasks) to his servants	Gives task and gifts to his servants (Acts 2, Ephesians 4:6ff)
Kingdom rule rejected by some	The message would be to Israel first who rejected the kingdom offer
Master returns	This Jesus shall come
Judges and destroys the rebellious citizens	Vindication is implied by the fact that they were to be his "witnesses" (martyrs), his return would be their vindication (cf. Revelation 6, 11)

Based on these perfect parallels, the question must be asked: what is the difference? What is the hermeneutic that demands that we see two different comings - two different "bodies" - for two different reasons?

There is yet another connection here that Dan Dery develops earlier in this work, and that is that the scene in Acts 1 is sacerdotal, meaning, it is "priestly" in nature. We simply cannot overlook or ignore the fact that Jesus was acting as the Great High Priest, about to enter the Most Holy Place. The priestly connection is fully confirmed when we remember that Acts 1 is the ascension of Christ to the right hand of the Father in fulfillment of Psalms 110. And in Psalms 110, we are told: "you are a priest forever after the order of Melchizedek." Since Psalms 110 conflates the Sovereignty of Messiah on the throne with the priesthood of Messiah, then in the Ascension we must see Christ's actions as not only kingly, but priestly as well. This conjoining was predicted in other prophecies:

> *"Yes, He shall build the temple of the Lord. He shall bear the glory, and shall sit and rule on His throne; so He shall be a priest on His throne, And the counsel of peace shall be between them both."* (Zechariah 6:13)

Here, we have Messiah building the temple, which is echoed in John 14, where Jesus said he was going away to prepare a place "in my Father's house" which is nothing less than Temple imagery. Then, we have Messiah being both King and Priest on the throne. So, when Jesus, the Nobleman, ascended to the right hand of the Father in Acts 1, he was not only taking his place as King, but, he was ascending as High Priest. Thus, Dan Dery's focus on the Priestly nature of the Ascension must be honored. And this brings Hebrews into focus. In Hebrews 1:1-2, the writer says that Christ had operated as Priest prior to his ascension and enthronement. Speaking of how the Father had exalted him, the writer says of Christ:

> *"Who being the brightness of His glory and the express image of His person, and upholding all things by the word of His power, when He had by Himself purged our sins, sat down at the right hand of the Majesty on high, having become so much better than the angels, as He has by inheritance obtained a more excellent name than they."* (Hebrews 1:2-4)

So, acting as High Priest, Christ had offered himself. Acting as High Priest he ascended to the Father, to enter the Most Holy Place where the Mercy Seat was, there to offer his life:

> *"Therefore, it was necessary that the copies of the things in the heavens should be purified with these, but the heavenly things themselves with better sacrifices than these. For Christ has not entered the holy places made with hands, which are copies of the true, but into heaven itself, now to appear in the presence of God for us."* (Hebrews 9:23-24)

Notice Hebrews 8:1-2:

> *"Now this is the main point of the things we are saying: We have such a High Priest, who is seated at the right hand of the throne of the Majesty in the heavens, a Minister of the sanctuary and of the true tabernacle which the Lord erected, and not man."*

The priority of Christ's priesthood is an important fact, especially in light of Dery's development above. We simply must view Acts 1 as the outplaying of Christ's High Priestly praxis. And, since Hebrews 8 clearly identifies that work as heavenly and spiritual - not "earthly" or physical - this is highly suggestive that his return would be in agreement with that, that is, of the same heavenly/spiritual nature. One thing is simply undeniable: the writer of Hebrews expected that coming out of the MHP to occur soon. Look at what Hebrews 10:35-39 had to say:

> *"Therefore, do not cast away your confidence, which has great reward. For you have need of endurance, so that after you have done the will of God, you may receive the promise: "For yet a little while, And He who is coming will come and will not tarry. Now the just shall live by faith; But if anyone draws back, My soul has no pleasure in him." But we are not of those who draw back to perdition, but of those who believe to the saving of the soul."*

So, the writer of Hebrews urged his audience to faithfulness, urging them not to return to the Law and its cultic, festal observances. Their (great) reward was at hand and it was coming "in a very little while." It is to be noted that the Greek here is extremely powerful. It is:

γὰρ, (for), mikron (Μικρὸν, A little), (hoson, ὅσον) very, hoson ὅσον), - notice the repetition of "hosan," giving us the meaning "very, very little," while, (ho, ὁ- the), the [One], erchomenos, (ἐρχόμενος, coming), hēxei, (ἥξει, he will come), kai, (καὶ, and), ou, (οὐ, not), chronisei, (χρονίσει, delay).

So, the writer said that in "a very, very little while," the "coming one" will come, and he will not delay. Who was the "coming one"? It was, of course, Christ, the Great High Priest, who was coming, "to those who eagerly looked for him" (Hebrews 9:28). It was the Great High Priest coming out of the Most Holy to consummate and bestow the Atonement blessings on the waiting audience. Of course, there is no question that Hebrews 9:28 - and thus, Hebrews 10 - are the same coming of the Great High Priest to bring salvation as promised in Acts 1. (Would anyone doubt that?) With these connections in mind, please consider the following:

-The coming of Christ in Acts 1, is the coming of Christ of Hebrews 9:28, his coming as the Great High Priest to bring salvation - consummating the Atonement.

-But, the coming of Christ of Hebrews 9:28, his coming as the Great High Priest to bring salvation - consummating the Atonement was – from the perspective of Hebrews - coming "in a very, very little while and without delay.

-Therefore, the coming of Christ in Acts 1, the coming of Christ of Hebrews 9:28, his coming as the Great High Priest to bring salvation - consummating the Atonement was from the perspective of Hebrews - coming "in a very, very little while and without delay.

Furthermore, since the coming of Christ in Acts 1 is his coming to "put down the last enemy" at the time of the resurrection in fulfillment of Psalms 2, Psalms 110, 1 Corinthians 15, this means that Christ's coming as the Great High Priest to bring salvation - in fulfillment of Psalms 2, Psalms 110, 1 Corinthians 15, was - from the perspective of Hebrews - coming "in a very, very little while and without delay.

I suggest that Christ's priestly ascension to the Most Holy Place (Hebrews 9:23f) was also his departure as the Nobleman to go to the far country, there to receive the kingdom and to return. Notice that upon his return in Luke 19, that the King gives gifts and blessings to his faithful citizens, just as the High Priest brings salvation to those who look for him. We thus see the conflation of "King and Priest" just as Zechariah 6 and Psalms 110 anticipated.

All of this evidence demands a re-examination of Acts 1 and the promise of the return of the King as the Great High Priest. If it is true that the coming of Christ in Acts 1 and the coming of Christ in Hebrews is the same - and few, if any doubt it - then we have extremely powerful evidence and proof that Acts

1 was to be fulfilled in the first century. Unless therefore, one is able to prove definitively that Acts 1 and Hebrews speak of different comings of "the one who is coming," the one who is coming for salvation, the one coming out of the MHP, then we must, in spite of church history, the early church writers and the creeds, admit that Christ's coming, his "second coming", was in fact accomplished in the first century.

Bibliography

Preston, Don K. *Like Father Like Son on Clouds of Glory*. Ardmore, Oklahoma: JaDon Management Inc., 2006.

Terry, Milton. *Biblical Apocalyptics: A Study of the Most Notable Revelations of God and of Christ*. Grand Rapids: Baker Book House, 1898.

THE MEANING BEHIND THE MANNER

A COVENANT UNDERSTANDING OF THE ASCENSION OF CHRIST

DANIEL DERY

Made in the USA
Coppell, TX
18 December 2021

69310936R00056